CLASSIC
MOTORCYCLES

CLASSIC
MOTORCYCLES

MICK WALKER

CHARTWELL
BOOKS, INC.

Published by
CHARTWELL BOOKS, INC.
A Division of **BOOK SALES, INC.**
110 Enterprise Avenue
Secaucus, New Jersey 07094

Produced by
Brompton Books Corp.
15 Sherwood Place
Greenwich, CT06830
USA

ISBN 1-55521-736-2

Printed in Hong Kong

PAGE 1: *A 1954 BSA Golden Flash*

PAGES 2-3: *The 1973 world champion Phil Read on a 500cc MV Agusta.*

THIS PAGE: *Walter Villa aboard a classic Harley.*

CONTENTS

AMERICA

The American-made motorcycle is strictly a twentieth century phenomenon. There had been some investigation into the idea of a power-driven, two-wheeled vehicle in America prior to the turn of the century but the first commercially produced motorcycle in the United States, by the E R Thomas Motor Company, did not appear until 1901. Later the same year George Hendee, a former bicycle racing champion, and Oscar Hedstrom teamed up to manufacture motorcycles under the Indian name in Springfield, Massachusetts. Their design was considerably more advanced than the Thomas, with the Indian engine featuring inlet-over-exhaust (ioe) – often termed F-head in America. A popular color choice for the Indian was red – well it had to be, didn't it?

A concern in those early days of metallurgy was premature exhaust valve failure. In ioe engines, the idea was that the exhaust valve could be prevented from getting over-hot by locating the relatively cool inlet valve just above it.

Also in 1901 William S Harley and his schoolboy friend Arthur Davidson (both in their early twenties) were working for the same company in Milwaukee, Wisconsin: Harley as a draftsman and Davidson as a pattern maker. Another draftsman employed at the plant was a recent German immigrant, a man who had some knowledge of the De Dion petrol engine which had been developed late in the 1890s and was being copied throughout Europe for use in both cars and motorcycles. Harley had gained earlier experience working in a bicycle factory and became interested in the concept of adapting a petrol engine to a conventional bicycle. He eventually designed a set of patterns for a small aircooled four-stroke engine. With the help of his brothers Walter (who worked in a

Kansas rail engineering works) and William (a toolmaker) Harley was finally able to build a prototype machine early in 1903.

The original engine proved underpowered and the frame too weak. So the 'team' carried out a redesign which saw the capacity of the single cylinder engine rise to 405cc and the frame strengthened. Three of these new bikes – called the Silent Grey Fellow – were built that year and proved so successful that it remained the premier production Harley for over a decade (with an increase to 550cc along the way).

The year 1908 saw rivals Indian catalogue their first v-twin models, a 600cc roadster and 1000cc racer. Harley Davidson, too, soon came up with their own v-twin, a 45 degree device which was to be the forerunner of a concept which is still in production today.

Other American pioneer motorcycle manufacturers included: Thor, Old Pierce, Yale, Flying Merkel, Excelsior and Crocker – and the fabulous four cylinder Henderson and ACE models. But it was to be Indian and Harley Davidson who dominated the Stateside motorcycling scene for the first half of the century.

America played a vital role in the evolution of motorcycle racing in Europe. In fact, many of the very earliest European races were won by either Indian or Harley Davidson machinery. Both marques also competed in the Isle of Man TT – Indians taking the first three places in the 1911 Senior event.

By 1913 American companies had attained an annual output of 70,000 motorcycles, a considerable number of which were exported to the European market. Then came the Great War which stunted these exports, although it did open a new door, with the American military authorities purchasing large numbers for the US

LEFT: *Harley Davidson, America's most popular marque. Here's a 1942 WLA 750 side valve v-twin, Harley's famous warhorse.*

RIGHT: *The famous Duo-Glide model first appeared in 1958. Its name came from the fact that it had suspension on both the front and rear wheels. Later (in 1965) it became the Electro-Glide with the addition of an electric starter.*

Army. Both the leading marques had large distribution networks; Indian alone having some 2800 dealers nationwide by 1916.

The situation changed after World War One, when the success of Henry Ford's Model T and other four-wheelers increasingly turned America's attention away from motorcycles to cars during the inter-war period. This did not happen overnight, but was a gradual process over a number of years. Both Indian and Harley Davidson continued their fight for what sales there were, with a number of new models including side-valve v-twins in 45, 74 and 80cu.in. displacements. Indian also used such evocative model names as Scout, Chief, Big Chief and Prince. There was even an inline four cylinder model. But however hard they tried even the combined talents of the Harley and Indian engineers and salesmen could not stave off a drastic fall in sales during the 1930s which swept the entire American motorcycle industry. By 1936 Stateside two-wheel enthusiasm was at an all-time low with only about 100,000 machines registered throughout the entire USA.

That same year Harley Davidson decided that it must come out fighting or risk total extinction. And so it introduced a brand new design of v-twin – the 'E' – soon nicknamed the 'knucklehead' due to the fact that viewed from the offside the Harley 'E' engine looked like a fist with protruding knuckles. And the name stuck, so that today it is known purely by its nickname. The knucklehead remained in production until as late as 1947 and was largely responsible for an upturn in the company's fortunes.

Meanwhile Indian was dropping further and further behind its great rival – eventually going out of business in 1954. Even this however was long after the majority of other American marques who had largely perished in those bleak interwar days.

World War II saw both Harley and Indian supply a vast number of machines to the American forces. Crosley, Cushman and Simplex also built wartime motorcycles.

American manufacturers confined themselves to the domestic market during the 1920s and 1930s, and consequently motorcycle sport developed along different lines form that found in Europe. America went in for the spectacular with an accent on power and speed, while European racing concentrated upon the skill of the rider. In America cubic capacity was king, whereas Europe witnessed the development of engines and frames to match the demands of exhilaration circuits such as the Isle of Man.

For many years Stateside sport was controlled by the AMA (American Motorcycle Association) – and it was the AMA who governed American racing, not the world body, the FIM (Federation Internationale Motorcyclists) as it was in the rest of the world. The AMA system's weakness was that no one rider was allowed to develop to his ultimate potential in one particular field. For example the Harley Davidson factory team would usually have six or seven riders, but none would be able to dominate the championship as there were so many diverse events during the season – flat-track, road-race, scrambles, American TT and so on.

The basic AMA ruling was that you started with a standard bike and modified it for competition purposes. A minimum of 100 machines of a particular type must have been made, you couldn't have more than two cylinders or four gears and a 750cc side-valve was regarded as the equivalent of a 500cc ohv model. Double overhead camshaft engines were banned altogether. Many observers openly accused the AMA of creating rules which helped Harley Davidson and Indian with their 750 v-twins.

Without doubt the most spectacular of the AMA's events was the one-mile flat track. The circuit was prepared from hard-packed dirt, machines had no brakes whatsoever, and yet they were often timed at over 120mph on the straights. About 40 yards before the corners the riders simply (!) chucked the whole bike in sideways and slowed down by drifting. To witness a man fling a 300lb plus Harley v-twin sideways at 120mph on the dirt was really something.

It was not until the early 1970s that Americans – now riding mainly Japanese motorcycles – rediscovered European-style racing. And with it came the upsurge of the Daytona Raceway, on the Florida coastline. Until the end of the 1960s Daytona, at first the original

'beach' circuit and later a specially constructed tarmac speed-bowl, was the domain of either the giant 750cc American v-twins or 500cc British singles and twins. Then came the really big event, the Daytona 200 miler. Organizer Bill French was largely the man who brought American and European style racing together. This in turn led to Americans becoming specialists in road racing, and by the end of the 1970s the USA had its first 500cc World Champion in the shape of Kenny Roberts, followed by a horde of superstars in the 1980s such as Spencer, Lawson and Schwantz.

On the production front Harley Davidson are the sole surviving American marque, and today are enjoying unparalleled success in the showrooms. After going through a poor patch in the 1970s Harleys are now back at the top, and to many they are just as much a part of American life as apple pie, ice cream or hot dogs.

FAR LEFT: *During the 1960s and much of the 1970s Harley Davidson operated a manufacturing plant in Varese, Italy, where small capacity machines were built. Walter Villa won four world racing championships on these small HD two-strokes.*

CENTER BELOW: *A side-valve KR750 Harley racer from the 1960s.*

TOP: *The 1955 Harley Davidson 125cc Hummer two-stroke was based on a prewar German DKW design.*

RIGHT: *American half-mile flat track racing. All the bikes are Harley Davidson V-twins.*

RIGHT: *Gene Church in action on his Harley XR750 racer during the Battle of the Twins event, Daytona 1986.*

BELOW: *A 1977 Harley XL1000 Sportster in San Francisco. It was one of the factory's longest and best selling models.*

ABOVE: *Boulevard cruiser:
Harley's 1200cc Electra-Glide
of the early 1970s.*

FAR LEFT: *Electra Glides cruise into the sunset on Main Street, USA, with their riders in traditional 'patrolman' helmets.*

LEFT: *Harley Davidson secured police contracts in the early days, and the forces of law and order still use their bikes today.*

BELOW: *Duo-Glides were first introduced in 1958 and were the first Harleys with both front and rear suspension.*

LEFT: *The archetypal 'crucifix' look silhouetted against the evening sky.*

RIGHT: *The transformation of the Electra Glide into the Tour Glide considerably improved handling.*

BELOW: *Serious customizing added to the weight of the Electra Glides and many consider these bikes to be the epitome of American riding excess.*

PREVIOUS PAGES: *The stark black paint scheme enhances the predatory looks of this 1979 XLCR 1000.*

LEFT: *A spectacular example of a customized Harley, with lots of chrome and gold to off-set the handpainted color scheme.*

ABOVE: *Devotees like these ensure that the two-wheel subculture lives on. And few would want to argue with them.*

ABOVE: *An elaborately customized chopper on Daytona Beach.*

RIGHT ABOVE AND BELOW: *Some owners resist the temptations of outrageous customizing and try to preserve their bikes in mint condition, with that 'just left the factory' shine.*

ABOVE: *A rather lurid XLCR1000 Cafe Racer – mean, moody, and highly collectable.*

LEFT: *The Super Glide of 1979, with convoluted factory exhaust headers.*

RIGHT: *The revival of the Springer front end worked remarkably well and was appreciated by nostalgia-buffs and new customers alike.*

FAR LEFT: *The Softail Springer suffered in the wet from a limited grip caused by a skinny front tire.*

ABOVE: *The arrival of the Sportster 888e in the early 1980s brought Harley ownership to the masses.*

LEFT: *For an extra cost, the Sportster could be converted to the more powerful 1200.*

ABOVE: *The Can-Am, a road racer built by a Canadian-American consortium.*

RIGHT: *An FXRS Low Glide displayed to perfection at Daytona 1982, the year it was introduced.*

FAR RIGHT: *A rather spartan shape on Daytona Beach, one of the few US beaches to permit vehicles.*

THESE PAGES: *Customizing Harleys is big business and a serious art form. There really seem to be no limits to the adornments used by Harley owners: engraving, gold-plating, even encrusting them with jewels. It is also possible to obtain factory-prepared 'customs', but it probably isn't as much fun.*

FAR LEFT: *The start of Santa Pod raceway, where the legendary Marion Owens is revving up his twin-engined drag racer.*

ABOVE: *A 250cc flat track racer with a Bombardier Rotax engine; this highly-regarded bike was marketed by Harley on behalf of Can-Am.*

LEFT: *Stunt rider Doug Domokos at the opening of Daytona 200.*

PREVIOUS PAGES: *The legendary Gene Church, who still races – and wins – on Harleys as he has throughout his long career.*

INSET: *Jay Springsteen, the stunt rider whose name became synonymous with victory during his heyday on the XR750.*

RIGHT: *The flat trackers line up for the Orange County Half Mile on the fastest dirt track in the USA.*

LEFT: *Stateside the Italian Aermacchi ohv flat single was sold as the Harley Davidson Sprint. This is a 1970 350cc example.*

BELOW LEFT: *A Harley Davidson XLR v-twin racer.*

RIGHT: *The engine of a 1924 Henderson Ace. The four cylinder 1301cc inline unit produced 11.9 horsepower.*

BELOW RIGHT: *A 1929 Henderson four. The marque didn't survive into the postwar era.*

ABOVE LEFT: *The legendary Indian Chief – with rider in appropriate dress. A classic among American bikes.*

LEFT: *The Indian Four; early models were based around* the earlier Henderson Ace design.

ABOVE RIGHT: *A 1942 military WD model Indian, circa 1942. Today these bikes are highly prized by collectors.*

GREAT BRITAIN

The twentieth century was just six years old, Edward VII benevolently ruled a widespread empire in a world at peace – kept that way largely by dreadnoughts and gunboats, Sam Brownes and Short Lee Enfields. In the capital, Hansom cabs still clip-clopped around clubland but in the mews of Belgravia and Kensington, coachmen were rapidly becoming chauffeurs. Henry Royce was building 'the world's best motor cars' and his partner, the Hon. Charles Rolls, was racing them and selling them to the nobility and gentry.

In a somewhat lower social stratum an ever-increasing band of enthusiastic motor-bicyclists had firmly established themselves as a fraternity as well organized as their more affluent, four wheel cousins. Founded on the lines of the Automobile Club of Great Britain and Northern Ireland (later the RAC), the Auto Cycle Club was their governing body; and it was to be at the Club's 1906 annual dinner that the first idea of a motorcycle Tourist Trophy was put forward.

Prior to this British riders and the fledgling motorcycle industry had to contend with stringent speed limits, first of 12 and later of 20 miles an hour, which were more than rigidly enforced by the local constabulary – as indeed was any regulation which would assist in clearing the highways of any unwanted 'horrors'. So while their Continental counterparts were able to organize speed events on their countries' roads the competitive spirit of British riders could only be satisfied on a handful of small cycle tracks which then existed. This, in turn, meant that the development of British machines suffered, for without the spur of competition under natural road conditions and only the artificial banked tracks to race on, the designers and manufacturers of the day had virtually no effective means of testing and developing their products.

The result of the ACC annual dinner of 1906 was to inspire a road race of major importance for *touring machines*, to be held the following year. The chosen venue was the Isle of Man and from this developed the greatest series of motorcycle races of all time – the legendary TT.

The Isle of Man was selected because the Auto Cycle Club had to look outside England for the reasons outlined above. Immediately the Club's thoughts turned to the Isle of Man; not only had it been the scene of its elementary trials to select the British team for the International Cup in 1905 but the Island had, and still has, its own government, which permitted its roads to be closed for racing. The success of this event not only meant that it is still running to this day, but coupled with another highly significant development, had the effect of raising the standard of both the sporting British motorcycle, and its touring counterpart too (although at that time the two were almost the same).

The other significant development was the opening of Brooklands – a circuit which few present-day enthusiasts know anything about other than the name. This magnificent 2.75 mile banked concrete saucer, not used since the outbreak of the Second World War, was for 32 years the scene of hundreds of races, thousands of successful record attempts and countless hours of testing by British

LEFT: *Colorful AJS advertising poster from 1950. It displays the company's involvement in all forms of motorcycling illustrating both touring and sporting themes together with a quality image.*

RIGHT: *Throughout the 1950s and much of the 1960s AJS offered a series of big ohv singles suitable for one-day trials. These 'mud pluggers' were heavyweight and dependable, but were to be totally outclassed with the arrival of the new breed of lightweight two-stroke trials bikes such as the Spanish Bultaco and Montesa.*

LEFT: *The Selly Oak, Birmingham Ariel company had a proud and famous history and was one of the founding members of the British motorcycle industry. A 350cc Red Hunter of the mid-1950s is shown here on Douglas Head, Isle of Man.*

INSET LEFT: *Ariel singles were particularly successful in trials and scrambles. Here club rider Chris Kennedy leads a couple of other competitors at a pre-1965 event on a very rare 1957 500cc HT5 model.*

ABOVE *A sparkling big British parallel twin, the 646cc AJS model 31 CSR. This 1965 version was capable of around 110mph with excellent handling and braking for its era.*

Harold Daniell and Freddie Frith, who rode to victory on their AJS, Norton, Rudge, Sunbeam and Velocette machines, creating in the process an aura of invincibility of inestimable value to the industry they represented.

British designers were also instrumental in much of the country's success. These men included Ike Hatch, Doug Hele, Bert Hopwood, Val Page, Erling Poppe, Edward Turner and Phil Walker and many others of no less importance.

Continental manufacturers (and riders) led by Germany and Italy, tried all they knew to wrest supremacy from the Anglo Saxons, but largely to no avail. BMW and Moto Guzzi, however, both managed victories in the TT with German and Italian riders respectively.

Off-road, in the ISDT, British machines and riders were no less dominant than in racing during the interwar period, and in the lonely world of record-breaking there were yet more excellent performances.

When hostilities ended in 1945 Britain was at a low financial ebb. Quite simply virtually everything manufactured in the first few years of peace had to go for export to replenish the national coffers which had been so drastically reduced by six long years of conflict. The British themselves had to make do with either well-worn prewar models or reconditioned ex-military machines which were released on to the civilian market.

By 1950 the situation was stabilizing and new designs, previously only available to foreign buyers began to be available at home. Included among these newcomers were the likes of various small capacity two-strokes such as the BSA Bantam and several marques with Villiers engines; the BSA 500 Star Twin (soon followed by the larger 650 Golden Flash); Norton Dominator Twin; Sunbeam S7 and S8; Triumph 6T Thunderbird; Velocette MAC and MSS singles, and perhaps the most glamorous machine of its era, the Vincent HRD v-twin.

These models, together with later variations of the basic design continued to be the mainstream of British production roadsters

ABOVE: *The BSA M20 military bike saw widespread use by the British army during the Second World War. Powered by a 496cc single cylinder side-valve engine, well over 100,000 examples were produced for the war effort.*

RIGHT: *Ariel described their 1000cc Square 4 as 'Whispering Wildfire'. A more accurate term was 'The Gent', which one particular tester of the period labelled it. The Mark 2 shown here was offered between 1953 and 1959.*

throughout the decade, which peaked in 1959 with record registrations of some 300,000 units on the home market. From then on it was unfortunately downhill all the way through the 1960s, until at the beginning of the 1970s only the BSA group (including Triumph) and NV (Norton Villiers – following the collapse of AMC, which included AJS, Matchless, Norton, James and Francis Barnett in 1966) were left. By the mid-1970s BSA were also gone, and only NVT (Norton, Villiers, Triumph) survived. The mighty industrial empire that had once ruled the motorcycle world was all but finished.

In the sporting ranks the end had come somewhat earlier. Racing development since 1945 had at first seen the dominance of British AJS, Norton and Velocette machinery. This included winning inaugural World Championships in three of the five classes in 1949 – 350cc (Velocette), 500cc (AJS) and Sidecar (Norton) – until 1952. Thereafter first the Italians and later the Japanese dominated the proceedings.

A similar pattern evolved in the ISDT with the run of British success coming to an end at Gottwaldov, Czechoslovakia in 1953. From then on the Czechs, together with the West and East Germans took over.

Only in scrambles (later renamed motocross) and one-day trials

did British success continue at world level in the 1960s – thanks in no small part to the tiny Greeves factory, which built some truly excellent off-road irons which could match the very best produced anywhere in the world during the early 1960s. British riding talent continued to shine in all forms of the sport until the late 1970s. Today, it is only in motorcross and sidecar racing that Brits seem able to produce regular championship material.

Finally, although much has been written about why the British motorcycle industry finally crumbled, it was *not* due, in the opinion of the writer, to its riders or designers, but in reality much more to the British industrial system where short term profits are the all important consideration, rather than a longer term approach that provides managers and designers a better chance of success in world markets. The fact remains, however, that Britain can rightly claim to have led the motorcycle field for more years than any other nation – something modern day riders may find hard to believe.

RIGHT: *Malcolm Hall high-flying his 500cc BSA Gold Star Scrambler. Bikes like this dominated off-road racing during the 1950s and early 1960s, when British big singles thumped their way around the circuit to many a victory.*

BELOW: *BSA DBD Gold Star 'Road Racer' in American trim, circa 1959. On both sides of the*

Atlantic this bike was highly prized by enthusiasts in the days before the Japanese took over – and still remains so today.

RIGHT: *The classic Gold Star engine, this is a 350cc ZB32 of 1952 vintage, an all-alloy beauty which was equally at home on the street or race track.*

BSA

"GOLD STAR" ROAD RACER

1958 GOLD STAR VICTORIES
include:
10 Mile National Championship
15 Mile National Championship
25 Mile National Championship
Dodge City Grand Prix
Tobacco Trail Classic
Ohio State Championship
Minnesota State Championship
many, many others

A superb high speed road cruiser, the famous Gold Star is equipped with a super-tuned engine of racing characteristics—*exactly the same* engine that BSA competition stars use in road racing and track racing events. Can be quickly converted to road racing trim. Dirt track racing equipment also available.

Equipment includes 8000 r.p.m. tachometer on twin mount with speedometer, racing cams, 1½" racing carburetor, racing type fenders, racing 190 mm. positive-cooled front brake, and ventilated racing rear brake. Brilliantly finished dark blue tank with chrome panels, chrome fenders, and many other chrome plated parts.

LEFT: *The A10 Golden Flash was an excellent touring mount and ideally suited to sidecar work. In the immediate post-war era many English families would have seen the country from just such a sidecar combination.*

ABOVE: *A 1968 works ISDT (International Six Days Trial) BSA 440 Victor. Based on the successful motocross design which took the World 500cc Championship with Jeff Smith up in 1964 and 1965, these machines offered an excellent power-to-weight ratio for a four-stroke.*

Based in Thundersley, Essex, Bert Greeves began by designing and selling invalid carriages for disabled ex-servicemen. From 1952 he built bikes, and although he made roadsters, the sporting bikes were most popular.

LEFT: *Club rider W G Wright during the 1963 Scottish Six Day Trial – note rock strewn terrain – his mount is a Greeves 24 TES Scottish.*

ABOVE: *A 1966 Greeves 250 MX3 Challenger motocrosser with optional Italian Ceriani front forks. It offered race-winning performance.*

RIGHT: *Final variant of the Greeves Scottish 'mud plugger' was the 1965 TFS shown here, it was to be replaced by a new breed of trials machine which would carry the marque name for another four years.*

ABOVE LEFT: *For almost half a century the famous Bracebridge Street, Birmingham Norton works' bread and butter was a range of lumbering large capacity singles. Typical of these is this 597cc Model 19S. Manufactured between 1954 and 1958 it was essentially a larger engined version of the famous ½-litre ES2.*

LEFT: *An immaculate 499cc Manx Norton at Leguna Seca, USA. It is one of the truly great British bikes of all time.*

ABOVE: *The early 1960s saw Norton launch the 650 SS. With a string of wins in long distance races for sports machines, including the Thruxton 500 Miler event, it quickly established a reputation for excellent performance and superb handling. Even so the American importers demanded, and got, an even* more potent machine. This was the 750 Atlas, built between 1962 and 1968. It was also sold on the home market from 1964.

ABOVE LEFT: *The Rickman brothers, Don and Derek, were successful scramblers who created their own motorcycle, the Metisse – French for a female mongrel. The first model was powered by a Triumph twin cylinder engine.*

LEFT: *Other Rickman Metisse dirt racers were powered by Matchless and BSA singles. One of the latter is being raced here by Roger French.*

ABOVE RIGHT: *Following their off-road achievements the Rickmans produced Metisse models for road racing and even street machines, typified by this 1970 roadster with a Royal Enfield Series II Interceptor engine. Very rare and very nice.*

RIGHT: *A more common Enfield, a 1955 350 Bullet. The company's trade mark was 'Built like a Gun'. The design is still built under license in India.*

BELOW: *For many years Triumph machines were successful in long distance trials such as the International Six Days. This 650 TR6 Trophy was campaigned by the famous American rider, Bud Ekins during the 1960s.*

RIGHT: *In November 1952 a brand new Triumph design appeared, the 150cc Terrier, with a unit construction ohv engine. A year later and the 199cc Cub made its debut. The latter was offered in a variety of guises including roadster, trials and scrambler.*

BELOW RIGHT: *A Triumph Cub engine. Widely used on both road and track, by riders around the world, its main advantages are low cost and ease of maintenance.*

ABOVE: *Triumph's most famous postwar model was without doubt the 649cc T120 Bonneville. A 1964 Thruxton model is shown; these were specially tuned versions built to win races such as the Thruxton 500-mile marathon.*

RIGHT: *Three cylinder powerhouse, the Triumph Trident (and its sister the BSA Rocket 3) were the machines to beat in Formula 750 racing in the period 1969-1971.*

FAR RIGHT: *A Trident with one of the specially constructed Rob North frames. Essential for the track, rare on the street.*

FAR LEFT, ABOVE: *The limited production Craig Vetter styled Triumph X75 of 1972. Only very small numbers were built – a true collectors bike, which commands high prices.*

FAR LEFT, BELOW: *The Hall Green, Birmingham Velocette factory was most famous for their range of large-capacity singles. Typical is this 500 V-Line of the early 1960s.*

LEFT, ABOVE: *Superb 350 KTT overhead cam racing motor. Note traditional black and gold Velocette paintwork on fuel tank.*

LEFT, BELOW: *Velocette enthusiast Ivan Rhodes piloting his KTT around the Isle of Man TT course. Such a machine was the first ever 350cc class road racing World Champion back in 1949.*

ABOVE: *The all-conquering 1948 Vincent Black Lightning. It was used for both road racing and record breaking. In the latter category Rollie Free and Rene Milhoux set new American and Belgian national records respectively.*

RIGHT: *Vincent 998cc v-twin engine. It was both powerful and reliable.*

LEFT: *Riders eye view of a 1954 Vincent Black Shadow. Note the massive speedometer, steering damper knob and twin filler caps on tank – the smaller one is for oil contained in the massive top frame tube which acted as an oil tank.*

BELOW: *The late George Brown was perhaps the greatest of all Vincent riders. Besides racing them in the immediate postwar era, he later built first Nero, and then Super Nero (shown), with which he broke a number of both British and World speed records during the 1950s and 1960s.*

GERMANY

The Germanic traits of precision and correctness, for ensuring that every thing fits and works to the very highest degree ensured that from the very start Germany's manufacturing processes proved ideal in the development of engines suitable to power vehicles. Daimler, Otto and Diesel are just some of the great pioneering names in this field in the very earliest days of the mechanical revolution which swept Europe during the late nineteenth century. In fact it is generally agreed that Germany gave the world the internal combustion engine.

Another first, this time exclusive to two wheels was the Hildebrand and Wolfmüller motorcycle of 1894 – the first such machine to enjoy relatively large sales throughout Europe. It was a four-stroke v-twin of almost 1500cc. The standard model had a maximum speed of 25mph, while a racing version built later was capable of around 45mph. Soon the Hildebrand and Wolfmüller faded from the scene, to be replaced by more modern and efficient machines manufactured by the likes of Adler (1902), NSU (1901), Triumph (1902), Bismark (1904), Dürkopp (1901), Goricke (1903) and Miele (1899). Of these, NSU soon established itself as a clear leader. The company had a thriving export market in Britain during the early 1900s and its manager there, Martin Geiger, rode one of the Neckarsulm bikes in the

very first Isle of Man TT race in 1907, finishing a creditable fifth in the single cylinder category. With the outbreak of war in 1914 NSU, together with the other leading marques, soon found a new outlet for their wares with the German military machine.

When the war ended in 1918 much of Germany's industrial might went through a very lean patch. But as the new decade dawned there came a rebirth of the economy. This in turn led to a vast increase in the demand for personal transport and the birth of several new firms offering motorcycles. Chief among these were BMW, DKW and Zündapp.

DKW was founded in Chemintz during 1920 by the Dane, Jorgen Skafte Rasmussen. By the late 1920s DKW had established itself as not only the largest motorcycle producer in the Reich, but anywhere in the world, having absorbed 16 other companies and employing a workforce of over 15,000. It produced exclusively two-stroke engined machinery (including cars!).

BMW had entered the motorcycle field through default. A major aero engine manufacturer during World War One, it had been forced into new areas under the terms of the Armistice. BMW's first entry into the motorcycle arena had been with a small capacity two-stroke (sold under the name Flink) and soon afterwards the

M2B15 493cc flat twin side valve engine, designed by Martin Stolle. Both these inaugural ventures proved less than successful, with the result that BMW's chief designer, Max Friz was asked to restore the company's pride.

Although Friz was really an aviation man at heart and hated motorcycles, there is no doubt that his work was that of a true professional. Unveiled at the Paris Show in October 1923 the new machine, the R32, created a sensation. Although it retained the flat-twin engine layout it now featured in-unit construction with shaft drive to the rear wheel. The frame was a full twin triangle affair and the front fork was sprung by a quarter-elliptic leaf spring. It was the beginning of a design layout which was modern enough to endure to this very day. Although the 1923 R32 was not as powerful as some of its contemporaries, the BMW design was superior in several important areas and offered a truly modern concept in a world still dominated by unreliable engines, flimsy frames and temperamental transmissions.

Zündapp had been founded in September 1917 at the height of the Great War to manufacture fuses for artillery guns. At the end of hostilities the new company struggled to replace its now redundant war materials. It was acquired in 1919 by Dr Fritz Neumeyer who preceeded to transform it into one of Germany's top motorcycle manufacturers. The very first Zündapp two-wheeler was powered by a British-made Levis two-stroke engine. Thereafter the Nürnburg concern went on to build its own engines, with both two and four-stroke power units.

The German motorcycle industry boomed throughout the 1920s. Then came the Wall Street Crash in October 1929 and with it the Great Depression, during which over 5½ million Germans were unemployed. Somehow the major marques, DKW, BMW, NSU and Zündapp, hung on and by 1933 the German economy was making a massive recovery. With this came a vast resurgence of sales and a

BELOW LEFT: *Adler was established in 1886 to manufacture bicycles. Its first powered two-wheeler appeared in 1902, but it was not until 1949 that it became a motorcycle maker in the full sense of the word. The first MB250 twin was launched in 1952, and became a trendsetter, influencing designers in both Britain and Japan.*

ABOVE: *BMW are the most successful marque in the history of the World Sidecar Championships, having won the title a total of 19 times betwen 1954 and 1975.*

BELOW: *The classic BMW R695 flat-twin, mainstay of the famous marque throughout much of the 1950s and 1960s.*

major impact by BMW, DKW and NSU in motorcycle sport, notably road racing.

During the late 1930s, whilst Auto Union and Mercedes Benz flew the German flag in the four-wheel circuit, their two-wheel cousins were attempting to achieve the same level of success, backed by a government striving hard for national prestige. This effort came to a peak in June 1939, when a BMW ridden by Georg Meier won the Senior TT – the first time in the history of the famous Isle of Man races that a foreign rider on a foreign machine had won this Blue Riband event.

After the Second World War, with Germany divided into East and West, another now famous German marque was born. This was MZ and it was manufactured in Zschopau – formerly the headquarters of DKW (who themselves had relocated after the war to the western sector). MZ followed in DKW's footsteps by producing two-stroke engines. Determined to improve this particular engine type, MZ, under the leadership of their chief engineer Walter Kaaden, developed a new rotating disc induction system. Applied to the traditional two-stroke power unit, this innovative type was to prove outstandingly successful.

MZ became the world leader in this particular type of engine design and by the end of the 1950s were making strong challenges for world honors in Grand Prix racing. Unfortunately not only did their top rider Ernst Degner defect to the West and later join the Japanese Suzuki team (who were to make full use of MZ-inspired technology), but MZ themselves were held back from ultimate success by political, rather than technical means. Normal production models were never to use the technical expertise developed on the track, concentrating instead upon the utilitarian 'ride-to-work' sector of the market place. Glory finally came to MZ and East Germany by way of the ISDT during the 1960s and 1970s.

Meanwhile in the more affluent West Germany, BMW, DKW, NSU and Zündapp had been joined by the likes of Kreidler and Maico to offer some excellent new motorcycles both for road and track during the immediate postwar era. The most successful in terms of sales was without doubt NSU, who, when output of the Quickly moped series was taken into account, were the largest manufacturers in the world during the mid-1950s. NSU were also outstanding during the same period in the 125 and 250cc World Championships. In fact Soichiro Honda, who later used Hailwood and Redman in his team, was to reveal that he had modeled his racing effort on that of the NSU team.

BMW – who were virtually bankrupt in 1959 – were not only to survive and become the dominant German car and motorcycle success story of the 1980s, but also won a record of 19 world sidecar titles, mainly during the 1960s.

DKW never quite regained their prewar eminence, but did have the satisfaction of creating a highly innovative two-stroke three-cylinder racing model during the 1950s, before transferring their interest to four wheels and ultimately being absorbed in the giant VW-Audi combine. In the latter respect NSU, who had enjoyed great success as an independent, were to suffer a similar fate.

Zündapp survived the mass of closures and takeovers which dominated the German motorcycle industry during the late 1950s, only for it to happen much later in 1984.

Of the modern manufacturers, Kreidler and Maico were the most notable. Kreidler produced vast sales of 50cc motorcycles and mopeds and dominated the 50cc world racing championship with a record-breaking seven wins. Maico ruled the off-road sport (Enduro and Motocross) from 1955 until the late 1970s.

Ultimately the German motorcycle industry (except for BMW) was to fail, ironically as a result of the postwar German economic miracles which provided the average 'man-in-the-street' with one of the highest standards of living in the world. With high-quality cars available to everyone, the Germans only needed motorcycles for pleasure or sport. Despite the excellent reputation of their machines, demand from overseas has still not produced enough revenue to restore the industry to its former glories.

BELOW LEFT: *Italian engineering genius Arturo Magni – former chief of the MV Agusta racing team – builds and sells a line of BMW engined sports bikes. The result is a unique and expensive masterpiece.*

RIGHT: *Introduced in 1976, BMW's R100RS broke new ground in providing riders with a highly suitable 'motorway express'. The fairing shape was finalized after extensive testing in a wind tunnel belonging to the Italian car styling specialists, Pininfarina.*

BELOW: *Perhaps the finest BMW flat twin, the 900cc R90S was an adept high-speed tourer.*

LEFT: *The German DKW marque was founded in 1920. Amazingly less than a decade later it could claim to be the world's largest motorcycle manufacturer. In the late 1930s its supercharged 250 and 350cc racers were just about the fastest and noisiest things on two wheels. One of the 1939 racers is shown here, beautifully restored.*

ABOVE: *After the war, DKW were forced to relocate to the West – their original factory had finished up in the Russian sector. Also supercharging was banned, so new 'Deeks' were designed, including this three-cylinder 350cc machine, which was raced between 1953 and 1956.*

BELOW: *The final works' DKW racer was this fully streamlined 350 triple. By 1956 it was capable of exceeding 140mph – a truly sensational performance for its time.*

ABOVE LEFT: *Another technically advanced German machine was the 1954 Horex Imperator. It preceeded very similar Japanese designs which appeared in the mid-1970s.*

FAR LEFT: *The Kreidler factory concentrated its efforts on the 50cc class, winning more world 50cc racing championships (7) than any other marque. Works' rider Stefan Dorflinger is shown here on his way to victory in the 1981 West German GP.*

ABOVE: *The Kreidler with which Hans Georg Anscheidt finished third in the 1964 title chase against the might of the Japanese teams. It employed a 49cc disc valve, two-stroke engine.*

LEFT: *German engineer Friedl Münch built the prototype Mammoth superbike in 1966. The 1970 'Daytona Bomb' was a specially tuned model for record breaking.*

LEFT: *MZ (Motorrad Zschopau) was built up from the ashes of the DKW factory. Its chief designer, Walter Kaaden, pioneered the modern two-stroke during the 1950s, only to see his work transform the results of the Japanese Suzuki concern when his top rider Ernst Degner defected at the end of 1961.*

RIGHT: *The East German MZ concern were also very successful in the world of long distance trials. Here one of their riders forces his machine through a hazardous torrent during the ISDT.*

BELOW: *Well over one million NSU Quickly mopeds were produced between 1953 and 1965, making it Germany's most popular powered two-wheeler of all time.*

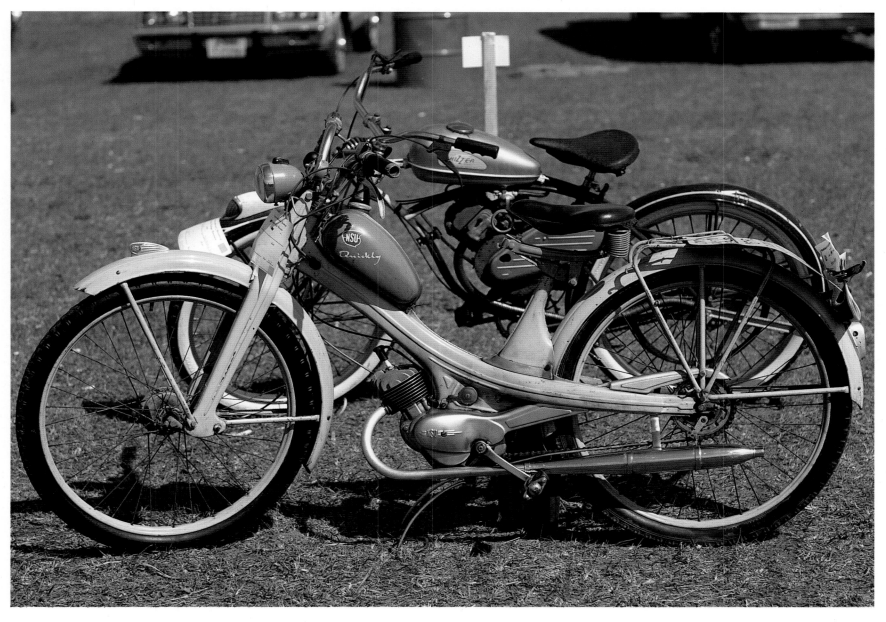

ABOVE: *In 1953 and 1954 NSU swept all before them in the lightweight racing classes with their Rennfox and Rennmax models. The factory then officially announced its retirement from the sport. However, a production-based Sportmax still managed to retain the 250cc title in 1955 ridden by Hans Peter Müller – a superb achievement.*

RIGHT: *The NSU Delphin Streamliner set a new world speed record at the Bonneville Salt Flats, Utah, in August 1956. Piloted by Wilhelm Herz, this projectile averaged 210.6mph. One of the prewar 500cc supercharged racing twins is in the background.*

INSET, FAR RIGHT: *Introduced in 1952, the 247cc NSU Max employed a unique method of camshaft drive using long connecting rods and levers housed in a tunnel cast integrally in the cylinder barrel. The same method was also used on the Sportmax racer.*

ITALY

For many years Italy lagged behind the majority of other major European countries in the early development of the internal combustion engine, and in particular on the racing side. Notably, France and Britain were the ones who led the way, both in the development of suitable machines – and the organization of events. In those pioneering days of the embryo Italian motorcycle industry around the turn of the century, one name was to loom large: Eduardo Bianchi.

Bianchi began his business career in 1885, at first manufacturing surgical instruments, followed by pedal cycles. Then in 1890 came his first motorized vehicle, a tricycle. Seven years later, Bianchi produced his, and Italy's first motorcycle. By the turn of the century Bianchi motorcycles were on general sale to an eager clientele and the Italian love-affair with the motorbike had begun.

The success of this venture encouraged others taking the plunge to become bike builders in their own right. These included Giuseppe Gilera in 1909, the Benelli brothers two years later in 1911 and the redoubtable Carlo Guzzi, who together with Giorgio Parodi, founded the Moto Guzzi marque in 1920.

Other notable entrants were Adalberto Garelli, who constructed his first machine in 1913, and started his own production line specializing in two-strokes in 1919; Mantovani and Rovetta with watercooled engines in 1902 and 1904 respectively; and Emanual Roselli who offered an extensive range of motorcycles from 1899 through to 1910.

It was not until after the end of the First World War that the first Italian racing machines began to appear, such as the Garelli two-stroke split single and four-strokes from Bianchi and Moto Guzzi. An important day in the history of Italian racing came on 7 September 1924, when the very first official European Championship meeting was staged at the Monza Aerodrome, near Milan. This was limited to 500cc machines and the chequered flag went to Guido Mentasi on a four-valve, horizontal Motor Guzzi single. Two years later Pietro Ghersi won the Junior TT on a 250cc ohc version of Moto Guzzi's single. It was a remarkably modern-looking chassis, though unfortunately Ghersi was disqualified for using the wrong spark plugs and thus lost the title.

Until this time it had largely been the British who had dominated racing, but thereafter Italy, together with several other European countries including Germany, began to put up a challenge. This Anglo-Italian rivalry reached a peak in 1935 when the legendary Irish rider Stanley Woods scored a famous Lightweight (250cc) and Senior (500cc) TT double mounted on a pair of Moto Guzzis – the first to have been achieved with motorcycles not manufactured in Britain.

The Isle of Man had first played host to the TT series in 1907 and it had rapidly developed into the world's premier motorcycle race. Italy had three similar events – the Targa Florio, the Savio Circuit and the *Circuito del Lario*. The latter was the nearest the Italians got to the Isle of Man Mountain course, the Lario being a 50 kilometer (31 mile) public road circuit twisting and turning throughout its entire length in a switchback of climbs, descents and ultra-tight hairpin bends overlooking Lake Como in northern Italy. The 'Lario' races began in 1921 and ran each year until the outbreak of the Second World War, except for two interruptions in the early 1930s caused by the Great Depression.

RIGHT: *Aermacchi was a famous aircraft company which switched to motorcycles at the end of the Second World War. Their most famous design was a horizontal ohv single, which was successful on both road and track throughout the 1960s. This is a 402cc racer with Mike Ward in the saddle.*

FAR RIGHT: *The 1000cc 3-cylinder Laverda Jota superbike of the mid-1970s. Capable of over 140mph, it was the fastest production roadster in the world when launched.*

Star performer of the series was the magnificent Tazio Nuvolari, who scored many victories, including four consecutive wins riding a works 350cc Bianchi double overhead cam single.

Another famous Bianchi rider of the period was Achille Varzi. Like Nuvolari, Varzi won equal fame for his four-wheeled exploits. This was quite a feature of the Italian racing scene in the interwar years with Piero Taruffi of Gilera being another master of both crafts. In addition Enzo Ferrari ran a motorcycle racing team in the early 1930s – using British Rudge and Norton machines.

The late 1930s belonged very much to the 'big four' of Bianchi, Benelli, Guzzi and Gilera. Based at Arcora a few kilometers from the industrial sprawl of Milan, Gilera took on board a four-cylinder design called the Rondine in early 1936. The origins of this machine could be traced back to the year 1923 when a pair of young engineers, Carlo Gianni and Piero Remor, sat down and sketched a revolutionary new engine. A feature of this design was the concept of placing four cylinders across the frame, and so solving at a stroke the problems of cooling and drive which had long plagued the earlier inline types. The Rondine (originally called the OPRA) was a truly innovative piece of engineering which was to set the standard for the future postwar era, not just in Italy, but around the world. Besides Gilera, MV Agusta, and Benelli the majority of Japanese companies were to employ the layout with great success both on road and track.

In 1937 the Guzzi rider Omobono Tenni became the first Italian on an Italian bike to win an Isle of Man TT, when he took the Lightweight event. By 1939 Bianchi, Guzzi and Gilera had been joined by Benelli at the highest level of competition, and a Benelli (ridden by the Irishman Ted Mellors) won the Lightweight TT.

Guzzi, Gilera and Bianchi all constructed supercharged machines – the Guzzi was a blown version of their existing 250cc single; whilst Gilera and Bianchi both came up with 500cc fours, the latter an entirely new design. Benelli were also set to join the fray with their own four cylinder model which had a displacement of 2500cc, but the progress of these exciting designs was brought to an abrupt halt with the outbreak of war.

On the production side, other well known marques which helped establish the Italian industry during the interwar period included Aquila, Borgo, CM, Della Ferrera, MAS, Miller-Balsamo, Sertum, Stucchi and Taurus.

After the war the Italians were able to resume peacetime production faster than anyone else who had played a major role in the Second World War. Of the really large companies, only Benelli's facilities at Pesaro had been extensively damaged during the con-

RIGHT: *The Benelli 750 Sei was the world's first production six-cylinder motorcycle. This was very much the creation of Alejandro De Tomaso who took over the ailing Pesaro factory in 1972. The 750 Sei made its entrance a year later.*

TOP RIGHT: *Benelli's first 250 four cylinder racer appeared in 1939, but the outbreak of war meant that it was never raced. Then in 1960 a completely new version sprang on to the scene. Over the next decade it was raced not only in the original capacity, but also 350 (shown) and 500cc versions.*

BOTTOM RIGHT: *Benelli's top riders included Dario Ambrosini (1590 World Champion), Renzo Pasolini, Kel Carruthers (1969 World Champion) and the great Tarquinio Provini. The latter is shown here parading one of the 1960s 250 fours during the 1985 Isle of Man TT week.*

ABOVE AND RIGHT: *Bimota was formed in 1973 by three men, Bianchi, Morri and Tamburini, the initial and second letters of their names forming the company's name. Their first products were mainly frame kits. They later transferred into the manufacture of complete machines, first for the race circuit and later the street. Typical was the HB3, powered by a 1100cc Japanese Honda four-cylinder engine shown here in both static and action guises.*

flict. In a country starved of personal transport for almost six years, everything on wheels which came off the production line was snapped up like hot cakes in those first few months of peace.

The old established marques such as Bianchi, Guzzi, Gilera and MM mainly offered updated prewar designs – except for the tiny Guzzi Motoleggera 65cc two-stroke which soon made itself the most popular motorcycle in Italy. Other early sales successes included the Ducati Cucciolo and Garelli Mosquito micro-motors, as well as the hugely popular Lambretta and Vespa scooters.

The first postwar Milan show was staged in December 1946, at which several brand new designs made their entrance. Noteworthy among these was the futuristic fully-enclosed Miller-Balsamo Jupiter, with a 248cc ohv four-stroke engine. The remainder of the 1940s saw the industry rapidly establish itself as a major force on the Italian industrial scene, with a flood of new marques, such as Parilla, MV Agusta, Rumi, Mondial, Aermacchi, Capriolo, Motom and Morini. These newcomers and many other marques used part of their sales revenue to fund a comprehensive attack on the sporting front, including not only racing but trials and motocross.

Italian bikes and riders made their mark from the very first year of the new World Championship racing series (1949), with Nello Pagani (Mondial) becoming the 125cc title holder and Bruno Ruffo (Guzzi) taking the 250cc Championship. From then until the 1980 season, the combination of Italian motorcycle and Italian rider scored another 42 world road racing championships – plus many, many more by either bike or rider alone. The most successful marque was MV Agusta – and machines from them are listed in the *Guiness Book of Records* as the most successful in the history of motorcycle racing. With a total of 15 individual world titles, Giacomo Agostini is the rider to have gained the highest number of titles in the history of the sport.

By 1959 there were well over 3½ million powered two-wheelers on Italy's roads, making it the foremost motorcycling nation in Continental Europe. However, this was to prove the peak, with sales and therefore registrations falling over the next decade due, in no small part, to the arrival of the affordable small car.

The 1960s witnessed the closure of many leading firms including Rummi, MM, Capriolo, Bianchi, Parilla, and Motem. In addition, both Guzzi and Gilera had to be bailed out. Italian industry underwent a reversal of fortunes during the 1970s, some of the highlights being the introduction of excellent large-capacity machines by Benelli, Ducati, Guzzi, Laverda and MV Agusta. Import restrictions imposed on foreign bikes under 400cc greatly helped this recovery process, and is in stark contrast to the final decline during the same period of the once-great British motorcycle industry.

LEFT: *Viewed by many as the ultimate small capacity Italian sports roadster, the 1964 Ducati Mach I had a 248cc bevel driven overhead cam engine, and was good for a shade over 100mph.*

RIGHT: *Another much-loved early Ducati single-cylinder model was the 203cc Elite of 1959.*

BELOW: *Later, in 1968, Ducati carried out a substantial redesign of their single cylinder range. The result being a heavier frame and more robust engine. This is a 1974 239cc Mark 3.*

OVERLEAF MAIN PICTURE: *Determination written over every feature, Englishman Anthony Ainslie sweeps his home-tuned 250 Ducati to victory in a classic racing event. These Bologna-built bikes offer riders good levels of performance and reliability.*

OVERLEAF INSET: *The v-twin Ducati also makes an ideal racing bike as Malcolm Tunstall proves by taking his 750SS to victory in the Twin Cylinder class at Daytona in 1982.*

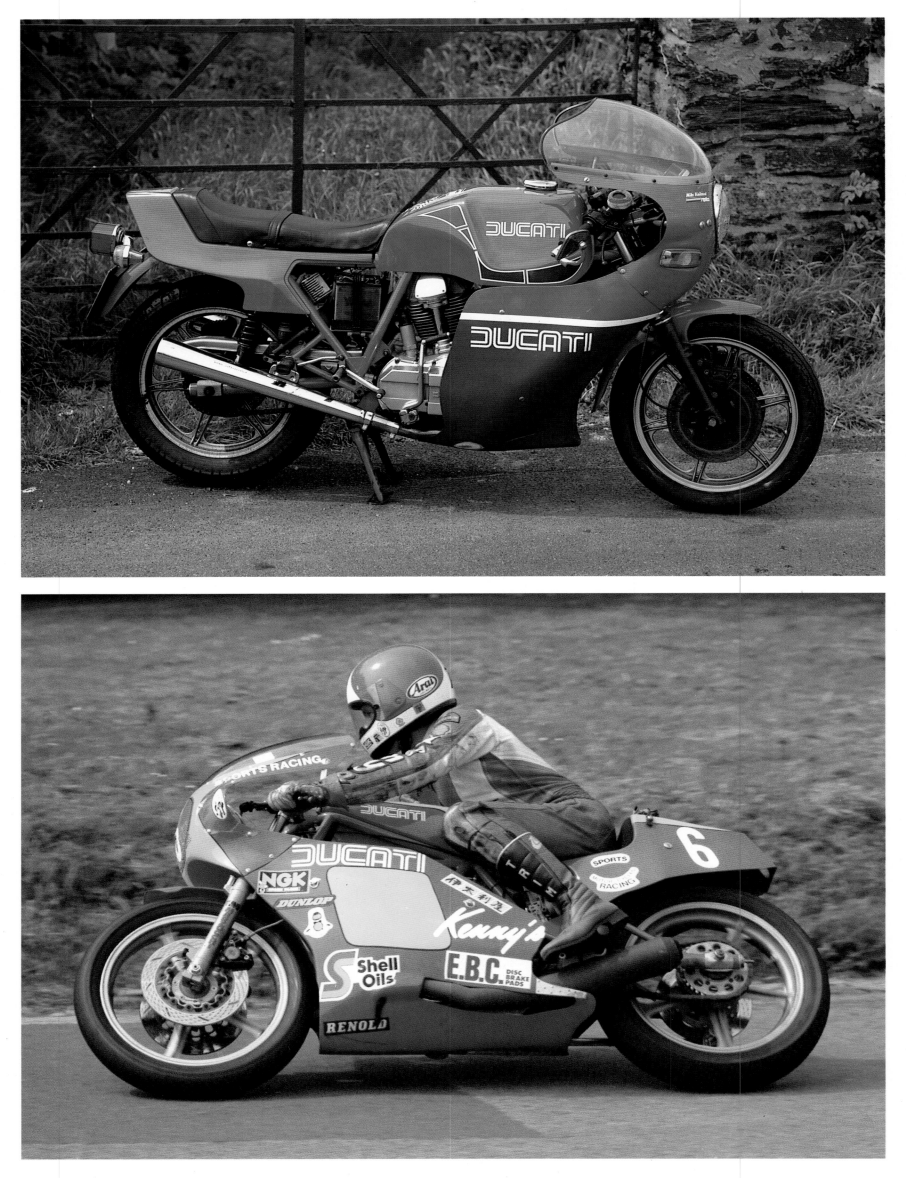

ABOVE LEFT: *In 1978 Mike Hailwood created a sensation by winning the Formula 1 Isle of Man TT on a Ducati v-twin after several years away from the sport. The factory cashed in on this success by creating the Mike Hailwood Replica sportster which went on sale the following year.*

BOTTOM LEFT: *Another success story for Ducati was Tony Rutter's four 600TT Formula 2 world championships during the early 1980s on a tuned version of what was essentially the Pantah roadster.*

ABOVE: *Designed in 1939, the Gilera Saturno did not enter production until 1946, thereafter appearing in roadster, road racing (shown) and even motocross forms.*

RIGHT: *The legendary Geoff Duke rode for the Gilera factory from 1953 till 1957. The Maestro is seen at the weigh-in for the 1954 Senior TT.*

LEFT: *Bob McIntyre created history by becoming the first man to lap the famous TT circuit at over 100mph on his Gilera four, while winning the 1957 Senior TT.*

TOP: *A Laverda 1000 RGS of 1982. based firmly on the original design of a decade before – three aircooled transverse cylinders – it provided a wide spread of power and high performance.*

ABOVE: *Final development of Laverda's big triple, the SFC 1000 of 1985 – a classic bike which could almost match the latest Japanese crop of racer replicas in the performance stakes.*

ABOVE: *Giancarlo Morbidelli was a successful industrialist who had a passion for fast motorcycles and created his own racing team. One of his leading riders was the 1977 250 World Champion, Mario Lega.*

RIGHT: *A Bologna-built Moto Morini racer from the early 1960s. The factory's best year was 1964, when it just missed winning the 250cc world title. Their top riders were Tarquinio Provini and Giacomo Agostini.*

FAR RIGHT: *Morbidelli rider Paoli Pileri en route to victory in the 1978 250cc Belgian GP. The disc valve two-stroke twin-cylinder engine pumped out almost 70 bhp and was good for 160mph.*

LEFT: *Moto Guzzi was born during wartime conversations between World War One pilots Giorgio Parodi and Giovanni Ravelli and their mechanic/ driver, Carlo Guzzi. Their first prototype appeared in 1919 and like this 1950s Falcone, was a 500cc horizontal four-stroke single.*

BELOW LEFT: *Dickie Dale taking a V-8 Guzzi to fourth place in the 1957 Isle of Man Senior TT – on only seven cylinders. This machine is regarded by many as the greatest racing motorcycle of all time.*

RIGHT; *The famous English rider John Surtees and his mechanic prior to the 1959 Senior TT which he won at record speed on his MV Agusta.*

OVERLEAF MAIN PICTURE: *MV Augusta star Mike Hailwood with broken screen during the 1965 Senior TT. He had earlier crashed, but remounted and went on to win.*

OVERLEAF INSET: *Champion of the Lightweights; Italian Carlo Ubbiali gained a total of nine world titles, the majority on MV machinery.*

BELOW: *Motor Guzzi set new standards for touring motorcycles when it introduced the automatic V-1000 Convert in 1975.*

LEFT: *With 15 World Championships and 123 Grand Prix victories Giacomo Agostini has scored more than anyone in the history of the sport.*

ABOVE: *When the MV Agusta 600 four-cylinder made its debut at the Milan Show in December 1965, it created a sensation, but in the years thereafter very few were actually produced.*

RIGHT: *The superb MV 750S of the early 1970s. It offered both speed and style in abundance – but at a high purchase price.*

TOP: *Extremely rare (only six were made) Parilla 175cc Bialbero (double camshaft). It was designed for Italian Formula 2 racing and used during 1956/57.*

ABOVE: *The very special Magni – MV Agusta four. Features include chain drive, square section swinging arm and 4 into 1 exhaust.*

RIGHT: *The definitive MV four-cylinder roadster, the 750 America of 1977. It exudes authority and breeding even when stationary.*

JAPAN

The first machine which could be classified as a motorcycle was imported into Japan from Germany in 1899. This steam-powered device with a pair of large wheels shod with solid rubber tire and sporting a pair of tiny auxiliary wheels was to set the land of the rising sun on the road to its present position as the dominant force in the world of motorcycling.

There followed a period where more conventional internal-combustion-engined motorcycles were taken to Japan by foreigners between 1901 and 1905. In 1907 a Japanese trading company began to import a quantity of British Triumphs. This same year also witnessed the first motorcycle racing over a bridle path which encircled Veno's Shinobazu Lake. This was quickly followed, in 1908, by the appearance of the first Japanese motorcycle engine, designed and built by Narazo Shimazu.

Shimazu's design was to inspire several more efforts, which included complete machines, usually with imported engines or frames. Although mainly of British origin, there were also NSU and Progress from Germany, and Indian from America. Finally in 1909 the Japanese government brought in laws which made it possible to import several foreign marques on a commercial footing, which effectively halted interest in domestically built products.

The first all-Japanese 'production' bike appeared in 1913. Built by Miyata, it was powered by a small two-stroke engine and sold under the Asahi (sunrise) banner, but generally the vast majority of local riders still opted for the more fashionable European and American machinery.

This situation continued to such an extent that although racing became hugely popular throughout Japan in the 1920s, its fledgling industry almost died. It was also during this period that Kenzo Tada became the first Japanese rider to take part in the Isle of Man TT races, riding a Velocette in the 1927 Junior (350cc) event.

When the economic gloom of the early 1930s finally lifted, the Miyata company resumed the manufacture of motorcycles in 1933 and, in April 1935, the concern began what could be labelled quantity production. The machine was a 175cc two-stroke single. Once again, this used the Asahi brand name, but unlike the previous effort, the new design proved a good seller. The major reasons for this were excellent performance and a good standard of reliability.

Foreign motorcycle competitors visited Japan for the first time in 1934. All five riders were Americans, headed by the well-known Pitt Mossman, who together with the others, had been invited to the

RIGHT: *The Japanese began their invasion of the European motorcycle scene in the early 1960s. On the race circuit Honda led the way – as they did out on the street. The company's stand at the 1964 London Earls Court Show displayed their wares to good effect. In the foreground is a 154cc G95 touring twin. Other models include a 305cc CB77 (left) and a CS90 (right).*

FAR RIGHT: *Today Bridgestone are famous for their tires. In the 1960s they also made a range of excellent motorcycles; amongst them the highly innovative 350GTR two-stroke twin which features disc valve induction, pump lubrication and six-speed gearbox.*

country by the organizers of the Yokohama Port Festival Exhibition. Their success in front of vast crowds not only helped establish motorcycle sport on a previously unknown level within Japan, but made the Japanese manufacturers realize that at least in racing, their machines were simply not good enough.

With the rise of military power in Japan during the mid-1930s came a change in national priorities. From now until the end of the Second World War a decade later, the military rather than the civilian authorities effectively ruled Japan. Although the civilian population had been discouraged from buying foreign motorcycles, the reverse had been true of the Army. And from the early 1920s they had been using Harley-Davidson v-twins. The sales of these American machines were handled by the Sankyo organization and, following a fall in the value of the dollar against the yen in 1929, an agreement was reached whereby Sankyo built machines in Japan working from drawings supplied by Harley-Davidson.

At first bikes were constructed from American supplied parts, but by 1935 machines were entirely of Japanese origin. Further commercial developments led to the brand name Rikuo being used. Thus came about the rather strange fact that Harley-Davidson v-twins were used on both sides during the war which was to follow; some 18,000 license-built Rikuos saw service with the Japanese military authorities, mainly in solo form, but some sporting sidecars. Other totally indigenous machines which were also used during the war included Asahi and Meguro.

When the conflict in the Far East finally ended in the summer of 1945, Japan was a shattered country, with the vast majority of its production facilities and cities little more than masses of rubble. No one could have foreseen the rebirth which was to follow from this scene of utter destruction and, in its wake, the creation of the biggest economic miracle in modern history.

Many of the first generation Japanese postwar motorcycles were extremely crude and perhaps none more so than the type built by a certain Soichiro Honda using a batch of war-surplus petrol engines which had formerly been used by the military authorities to power small generators. But these exceedingly basic machines sold like hot cakes in an environment hungry for any form of personal transport. And so the first hesitant steps were taken towards Honda's ultimate emergence as the world's largest motorcycle manufacturer.

A series of events – including near bankrupcy in 1953 – was to see Honda come out at the top of a myriad of small manufacturers which had sprung up in Japan during the late 1940s and early 1950s. By the year 1960, Japan was manufacturing an amazing 1.4 million powered two-wheelers of which a large percentage were of Honda origin. This was in no small part due to the unparalleled success of the 50cc C100 Super Cub which had been introduced in October 1958; in its first full production year, 1959, an incredible 755,000 Honda Super Cubs were sold. Of course others had also prospered, notably Yamaha, Suzuki and Tohatsu.

In 1960 the Japanese began their export drive, which was greatly assisted by three factors; import restrictions on the home market; an enthusiasm for investment in the future rather than in making quick profits – best illustrated by the high level of research and development and the willingness to sanction an expensive Grand Prix racing budget in a quest for publicity through racing success; and finally the ability to create what the market wanted.

As long ago as February 1954 Honda had despatched a works-prepared 125cc racing machine to take part in the prestigious international Brazilian São Paulo meeting. The machine's subsequent poor showing did nothing to dampen Soichiro Honda's will to

succeed, and later that year during a European visit – in which he took part in the Isle of Man TT – he took a special interest in the highly organized, all-conquering German NSU team, modeling his efforts thereafter in a similar fashion.

Honda did not return to the Isle of Man for another five years, in 1959. A team of twin cylinder 125cc models, led by chief engineer Niitsuma and American adviser Bill Hunt (who doubled as a rider), gained considerable publicity by winning the team prize. This was only the start. Yamaha and Suzuki joined Honda when they returned to the TT in 1960, and although there wasn't a Japanese victory, the writing was clearly on the wall for all those who wanted to see.

All three Japanese marques quickly realized that besides technical wizardry they also needed top line riders – and this meant signing established western stars. For example Honda's 1961 team consisted of not only four Japanese, but also Jim Redman, Tom Phillis, Mike Hailwood and Bob McIntyre. The net result was the first Japanese world championship trophies and TT victories; Phillis and Redman became 125 and 250cc champions respectively and Hailwood chalked up an impressive TT double.

This was the springboard from which first Honda, quickly followed by Suzuki and Yamaha, and finally Kawasaki (the latter having swallowed up the old established Meguro company ont he way) simply steamrollered the opposition. There followed a frantic battle between the Japanese 'big four' for racing honors which saw the most amazing array of designs; from Honda's jewel-like 50cc dohc twin which revved to over 22,000rpm, to models with up to five or six cylinders for the 125 and 250cc classes respectively. Only in the 500cc and Sidecar categories did non-Japanese machines continue to prosper. Later this sporting expertise was extended to other fields including motocross, enduro and trials.

Meanwhile the European manufacturers, already outgunned in sporting events, also found themselves overhauled in the standard production sector. This was most obvious in the lucrative American market, where the Japanese sold a host of multi-cylinder models at highly competitive prices which appealed to the American consumer. The Japanese motorcycle boom of the 1960s attracted many newcomers with Honda again leading the way, typified by

their slogan: 'You meet the nicest people on a Honda'.

Only in the bigger classes did the Europeans and Americans (the latter in effect now meaning a single marque, Harley-Davidson) continue to offer a creditable challenge. But even this was severely dented when the first four cylinder Honda CB750s appeared in 1968. From then on nothing could halt the Japanese sales effort, which not only owed its phenomenal success to the high quality of its products, but also to an unsurpassed marketing machine. Other manufacturers could only look on in envy as the Japanese companies pumped out millions of motorcycles, which sold all around the world.

LEFT: *A race-kitted Honda CB77 roadster being put through its paces by Bill Snelling.*

BOTTOM: *In 1965 Honda debuted the CB450 'Black Bomber'. It was the first Japanese bike to challenge for the traditional enthusiast big-bike sales. Technical features included torsion bar*

dohc, ultra short-stroke and twin 32mm carbs. On the road this added up to a maximum speed of 104mph.

BELOW: *Mechanical work being undertaken on a Honda 250 six cylinder racer of the type used by Mike Hailwood to win the 1966 and 1967 World Championships.*

ABOVE: *The arrival in 1968 of Honda's CB750-4 ushered in the year of the Superbike. This is the original version of this historic bike, which provided for the first time a mass-produced four which the ordinary man could afford.*

TOP RIGHT: *For the 1970 Daytona 200 race Honda produced a small number of very special CR750 racers. Based around the standard roadster it wasn't the fastest bike in the race, but Dick Mann still managed to win a famous victory.*

RIGHT: *A decade after Honda launched the CB750, it came up with the CBX – a six-cylinder monster with dohc, 24 valves, 108bhp, 100mph in seven seconds and a top speed in excess of 130mph.*

A quartet of classic Kawasaki superbikes: RIGHT: *Team Yoshimura at work. Stateside action with a Z1 in the foreground.*

BELOW: *Fearsome 500 three-cylinder two-stroke Mach 3 H1. This is the original 1968 version.*

OVERLEAF MAIN PICTURE: *Riders blast away from the start of the Daytona Raceway, America's premier Circuit.*

FAR RIGHT, TOP: *Works rider with a 750 triple at Leguna Seca, USA.*

FAR RIGHT, BOTTOM: *Mick Grant sweeping his 'Green meanie' to victory in the 1978 Isle of Man TT.*

OVERLEAF INSET: *Kenny Roberts, America's first World 500cc Road Race Champion in 1978, a feat he repeated in 1979 and 1980.*

INDEX

Acknowledgments

The author and publisher would like to thank the following for their help in the preparation of this book: Mike Rose, the designer, Nicki Giles for production and Helen Dawson for the index.
We are grateful to Don Morley for the majority of the pictures, and to the following individuals and agencies for use of the pictures on the pages noted below.

Mick Walker: pages 2-3, 36 (top), 64 (below), 68, 71 (below), 76 (top), 82, 85 (below), 88 (below), 91 (top), 95 (below), 102, 104, 105 (top), 106, 107 (below), 108.
Gary Stuart: pages 14, 15 (below), 21 (both), 25 (top)
Andrew Morland: pages 22 (top), 29 (left & below)
Julian Mackie: pages 15 (top), 23, 24, 25 (below)
National Motor Museum, Beaulieu: pages 16-17, 22 (below)
Bob Jones Inc: page 29 (right)